Printed in Great Britain
by Amazon

OLYMPIA

In the year 776 BC, the first Olympic Games were held in a town called Olympia in Ancient Greece. Many years later, a boy named Olly grew up there, dreaming of being an Olympic champion. But first, he would have to be better than his arch-enemy, Spiro...

First Published by Orchard Books

Text & illustrations
© Shoo Rayner 2011

ISBN: 9798884716445

This Edition © Copyright 2024
No part of this book may be copied,
lent or resold in any form, without
the author's permission

The right of Shoo Rayner to be
identified as the author and
illustrator of this work has been
asserted by him in accordance with
the Copyright, Designs and Patents
Act, 1988

www.shoorayner.com

OLYMPIA

WRESTLE FOR VICTORY

Shoo Rayner

Chapter ONE

"Ow! That hurts!" Olly yelped, as his arch-enemy, Spiro, pinned his arm behind his back.

Spiro's dog, Kerberos, barked madly in Olly's ear. Olly felt helpless. Why couldn't he beat Spiro at wrestling?

Olly's dad, Ariston, ran the gymnasium in Olympia, the town where they lived. The world's greatest athletes came to the gym to train for the Olympic Games that were held in the town every four years.

Olly and Spiro worked at the gym, running errands and helping the athletes. They also learnt many sporting skills by watching the adults.

Next week it was the Boys' Wrestling Match. Olly was desperate to beat Spiro, and he dreamt of being an Olympic champion one day.

But Spiro was bigger and tougher than Olly, and he didn't stick to the rules of wrestling...

"Ha, ha!" Spiro laughed. "And how about this?" Spiro grabbed hold of Olly's nose and tweaked it hard.

"*Yow! Dat hurts,*" Olly spluttered, his eyes watering. "*I givid.*"

"You give what?" Spiro chuckled.

"*I GIVID!*" Olly yelled.

"But I can't understand what you're saying," Spiro drawled.

Olly jerked his head away and freed his nose from Spiro's grip. "I give in!" he shouted.

Spiro pushed Olly over, then bent down and whispered menacingly in his ear. "So you'll do all my jobs at the gym for the rest of the day, then?"

Kerberos, sensing the game was over, began licking Olly's face with his long smelly tongue.

"Yes!" Olly raged in frustration. "Just let me go and get your stupid dog off me!"

Spiro stood up, leaving Olly panting and aching on the floor. He tossed a parcel into the dust beside Olly's head.

"Your first job is to take this parcel to Simonedes in the library," he snarled. "He's old and creepy and I hate running errands for him."

"I'll still beat you at the Boys' Wrestling Match next week!" Olly yelled defiantly.

Spiro burst out laughing. "You and whose army?" he taunted, as he walked away. "Come on, Kerby. We don't want to hang around with weaklings like him, do we?"

Kerberos gave one last growl for good measure, then trotted off after his master. His tail wagged as if he were a sweet little puppy – not the mad, dangerous killer that he pretended to be!

Olly got to his feet and stretched his aching limbs. "It's always the same," he grumbled to himself. "If Spiro doesn't want to do his jobs, he beats me up and makes me do them instead."

Olly picked up the parcel and limped on his way. "I have to beat him at the Boys' Wrestling Match," he muttered, as he walked along the hot stone path to the library where he could find Simonedes. "Spiro's a year older than me *and* he's much stronger. I have to find a way to win!"

"You look like you've been fighting the Trojan army!" Simonedes laughed, as Olly entered the library. "Is Spiro making you run his errands again?"

Simonedes was the athletes' history teacher. He also looked after the books in the library.

He was the oldest person Olly knew.

His body was bent over and his face was wrinkled and brown like a walnut. His stiff white eyebrows grew like wild bean shoots.

But his bright blue eyes revealed a fierce intelligence and a quick, sharp mind.

"I've been waiting for this to arrive," Simonedes said, unwrapping the parcel that Olly had brought.

"What is it?" Olly asked.

"A new book..." Simonedes replied.

The books in the library were written on scrolls. Each scroll had its title marked on a tag that hung down below the wooden shelves.

"Ah, Archimedes!" Simonedes whispered, as he slowly unrolled the scroll and began reading. "Is it a new story?" Olly asked. Simonedes smiled. "No. It's about mathematics, by a great thinker called Archimedes."

"Oh! I like stories best," Olly said. "I like the stories you tell us at lunchtimes. Stories about the gods and all the tricks they get up to and fighting and wars and things like that. I'm no good at mathematics. I'm glad you don't need to be be clever to be an athlete.

"You do if you want to be the best," Simonedes laughed. "And talking of lunchtime, shouldn't you be laying tables by now?"

"Yikes!" Olly leapt to his feet and set off for the dining room at the gym where he and Spiro helped to serve the athletes' meals. "I hope you've got a good story for us later!" he called to Simonedes over his shoulder.

Chapter Two

Everyday, as the athletes ate their lunch, Simonedes told them stories. Everyone already knew about the gods and the amazing, magical lives they led, but no one told the stories like Simonedes did.

When Simonedes was in full flow, it was almost as if the gods had come down from Mount Olympus, where they lived, and were right there in the dining room.

"Long ago, the gods of Mount Olympus fought a terrible war against the mighty Titans, who then still walked upon the Earth," Simonedes began. "The Olympians won the war and the mighty god, Zeus, banished the Titans to Tartarus, the dark abyss beneath the underworld...

"But as a special punishment, Zeus forced Atlas, the strongest Titan of them all, to hold up the heavens on his shoulders so that the Earth and sky should always be kept apart."

Simonedes took a deep breath. "Meanwhile, Heracles, son of Zeus, had a mission to collect golden apples from the garden of Hera, as one of his twelve great labours.

Olly looked at the paintings on the walls of the dining room. One showed Atlas, holding up the sky. Next to him was Olly's hero, Heracles, wearing his lion cloak.

"But Atlas tried to trick Heracles," Simonedes continued. *Hold up the sky for me for a moment*, Atlas told Heracles. *I will fetch the golden apples for you.*

"As Heracles struggled to hold up the sky, he realised he had been tricked. Atlas never intended to carry the sky again now that Heracles had taken on his burden.

"But Heracles was as clever as he was strong. *Hold up the sky for me for a moment,* he told Atlas casually. *Something is digging into my neck. If I roll up my cloak and make a pad for my shoulders, it will be much more comfortable.*

"Without thinking, Atlas lifted the sky onto his shoulders so Heracles could fold his cloak. But Heracles did no such thing. He grabbed the golden apples and ran away as fast as he could, leaving Atlas to carry the sky on his shoulders for ever and ever, until the end of time itself."

"Wow!" Olly whispered to himself as he cleared away a stack of wooden bowls. He was gripped by Simonedes' story. "I wish I could be as strong and as clever as Heracles – then I might be able to get Spiro off my back!"

Just then, Olly felt a sharp pain as Spiro stuck his foot out and kicked him in the shin.

"Ow!" Olly tumbled head over heels. The bowls flew through the air and clattered noisily on the hard marble floor.

The athletes roared with laughter. Olly had never felt so embarrassed in his life.

"Oh, whoops!" Spiro pretended to be concerned and offered Olly a hand.

"Did you slip on something, Olly?" Olly grabbed Spiro's hand and tried to pull him to the ground. But Spiro was ready for him. He was much stronger. He twisted Olly round and pinned him to the floor, wrenching his arm up behind his back.

"You fall for it every time!" Spiro laughed.

The athletes were on their feet, cheering. "Come on, Olly! Do something!"

"Save me, Heracles!" Olly yelled.

The athletes howled with laughter. Olly had never felt so small and useless.

Only Olly heard Spiro as he leaned over and growled in Olly's ear: "You'll never be strong or clever like Heracles. You're weak and stupid like Atlas, and I am the sky on your shoulders. I'll be a burden on your back for ever and ever, until the end of time itself!"

Olly looked up and saw Simonedes smiling at him. He was tapping the side of his head. He seemed to be saying something. Olly watched the old man's lips as they formed three words:

"Use your brain!"

Chapter Three

Olly's jobs were finished for the day.

Nursing his aching arm, he leant against the doorway of the library. Simonedes was deep in concentration, studying his new scroll.

Olly cleared his throat and Simonedes looked up.

"Come to learn how to wrestle, have you?" Simonedes smiled.

"From you?" Olly almost laughed, but he stopped himself. Simonedes held his gaze with an authority that Olly had to respect. "But you can't learn wrestling from books," Olly said.

The old man's eyes twinkled.

"I may look old and bent, but I was the wrestling champion in my day."

"Really?" Olly couldn't imagine Simonedes wrestling. He would snap in two at the slightest touch!

"Come with me," Simonedes ordered. He led Olly to the wrestling gym where the Boys' Wrestling Match would take place next week.

He stopped in front of a carved plaque on the Wall of Fame. Olly had walked past it many times before. "Well?" Simonedes smiled. "What does it say?"

Olly read the carved words out loud: "*Simonedes. The greatest unbeaten wrestler of all time.*"

Olly stared at the carved face on the plaque and then looked at Simonedes. "It's you!" he exclaimed. Now Olly understood why Simonedes was so interested in wrestling!

Simonedes waved his hand at all the other plaques. Each one praised a famous wrestler.

NASTI NIK
MEAN AND
-HARD-

PIRATE PETE
NO HOLDS
BARRED.

"I wrestled with all these great competitors, but I used my brain," Simonedes explained. "I stopped wrestling while I was still the champion. The others carried on too long. I dedicated myself to learning instead and grew old and happy. It's a lot safer."

"I'll never beat Spiro," Olly grumbled. "He always gets me the same way: he twists me round and sits on my back. He's so heavy, there's nothing I can do!" Olly kicked the air in frustration.

"Use your brain!" Simonedes sighed.

Olly looked confused. "But...what do you mean?"

Simonedes rolled his eyes. "Well, if Spiro always gets you the same way..." He trailed off, leaving Olly to do the thinking.

Olly frowned and tapped the side of his head. He stared at Simonedes, hoping the answer was written on his face.

Then, as if a spark had lit a fire, a smile crept over Olly's face.

"Aaaah! I get it! If Spiro always gets me the same way..." he said, "then I should do something that's not the same – something different?"

Simonedes threw his head back and laughed. "Now you're using your brain!"

"So what should I do?" Olly asked.

"You're the champion. You should have all the answers."

"Archimedes has the answer!" said Simonedes. "It's all in my new book. Come outside, I'll show you."

Outside, Simonedes found a large stone. "Do you think I can lift that?" he asked.

"No way!" Olly laughed. He tried to move it himself, but it wouldn't budge.

Simonedes found a long wooden pole,

and a smaller stone.

"The smaller stone is called a fulcrum," Simonedes explained. "The pole is a lever."

First, Simonedes wedged the end of the pole under the large stone.

Then, with the pole resting on the smaller stone, he pressed down on the pole. The large stone moved!

"That's amazing!" Olly exclaimed Simonedes drew diagrams in the sand as he explained Archimedes' theories about levers.

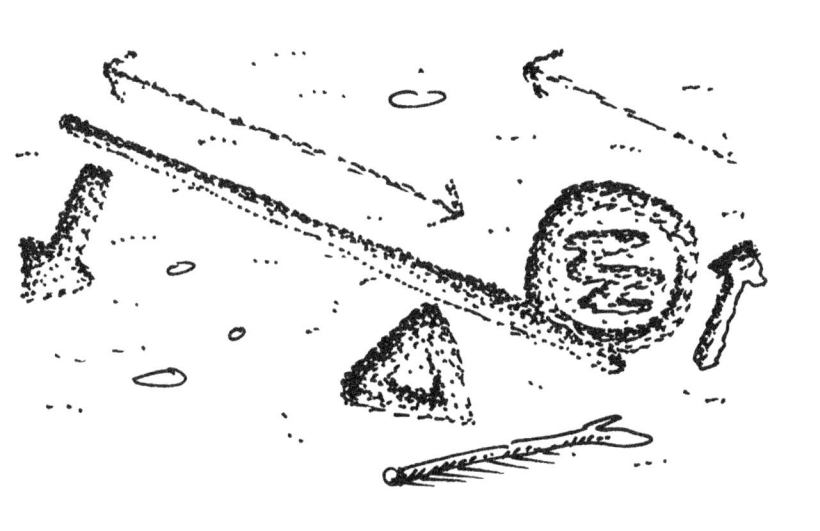

"Archimedes says, *Give me a lever long enough and I will move the world!*" said Simonedes.

"Give me a lever long enough," Olly smiled to himself, "and I can get Spiro off my back once and for all!"

Chapter Four

Olly and Simonedes spent the rest of the day discussing wrestling tactics. Simonedes drew pictures in the sand and explained how Olly could use his body as a lever to move Spiro, using Spiro's extra weight to his advantage.

"If he has you on the ground and he's sitting on your back," Simonedes explained, "you are helpless. That's where he always gets the advantage over you."

"So if he gets me onto the ground," Olly mused, "I need to flip over onto my back before he can sit on top of me. Then I can use my body as a lever"

Simonedes showed Olly a way of falling to the ground that was quick and didn't hurt.

"There you are," Simonedes smiled. "Now you're using your brain! Spiro only knows how to be a bully. You just need some skills and tricks up your sleeve to beat him."

Olly practised all week long. By the time the Boys' Wrestling Match came round, Olly felt more than ready.

Sport was the reason Olympia existed. Whenever there was a competition, half the town turned up to watch. Everybody crowded onto the wide stone steps beneath the Wall of Fame that enclosed the wrestling arena.

As other boys went through their matches, Olly paced up and down, limbering up and stretching, and rehearsing his new skills in his head.

Spiro leant against a pillar and smirked. He and Olly had been drawn to wrestle against each other many times before. Spiro wasn't worried. He knew he could beat Olly any day.

Finally, Olly's dad, Ariston, called the two boys to the centre of the ring. "Right, lads," he said. "We want a nice, clean wrestling match!" Ariston never showed any favouritism towards Olly, so Olly had to work just as hard at sport as the other boys.

Olly and Spiro looked at each other warily, eyes fixed, ready to grapple.

Thanks to Simonedes, Olly had learnt that his biggest mistake was to always make the first move. That was what Spiro was expecting.

Olly pretended to grab Spiro's hands, but this time he pulled back at the last moment. Spiro lurched forward and found himself grabbing thin air.

Olly dropped down and crouched at Spiro's feet. Spiro tripped and sprawled across Olly's shoulders.

Olly pushed himself up, hurling Spiro high into the air, where he turned a scrambling somersault before landing on his back.

"Oof! Why, you little…" Spiro snarled as he picked himself up from the floor. No one had ever done that to him before!

Spiro stormed up and grabbed Olly, but before he could twist him onto his front, Olly dropped and turned so that Spiro found himself sitting on Olly's chest. Spiro didn't mind – he was still on top, after all.

Spiro leant over Olly's face. His breath stank of garlic and goat's meat.

Olly was waiting for Spiro to lean over a bit too far, so he was off-balance – that's when he would be vulnerable and Olly could use Spiro's weight against him.

"Now!" Olly told himself. He pumped his legs, lifting his hips fast, launching Spiro off his chest.

Spiro sprawled forwards, landing on his chin. He was stunned for a moment, but a moment was long enough. Olly knew he had barely a second to get out from underneath and pin Spiro down.

He grabbed Spiro's arm and yanked it behind his back, just like Spiro always did to him.

"Yow!" Spiro wasn't used to losing!

"How about this?" Olly yelled, grabbing hold of Spiro's nose and giving it a good, hard tweak.

"Yow! *Dop id!*" Spiro yelled.

The crowd roared with laughter. They had never seen Spiro lose before. They sensed that Olly was moving in for the kill. This was a real wrestling match now, not just a big bully beating up someone smaller.

"Led go of my *doze!*" Spiro shouted.

"Do you give in?" Olly asked.

Spiro fell silent. He had never given in before, but he knew Olly had beaten him this time.

The crowd hushed. Spiro let out a small high-pitched yelp.

"What was that?" Olly demanded.

"I didn't quite hear you."

"*I GIVID!*" Spiro yelled.

"But I can't understand what you're saying," Olly taunted.

"Oh, yes, you can," said a firm voice behind him.

Olly felt himself being pulled off Spiro by his dad, Ariston. He winked and smiled at him as if to say, "*Well done, son, I'm so proud of you!*"

Ariston raised Olly's hand into the air. "The winner!" he proclaimed. The crowd erupted in applause.

They'd waited a long time for the day that Spiro was beaten by someone smaller and more skilful. Like Simonedes, the audience knew that skill and learning was always better than brute force.

As Olly accepted his applause, he caught Simonedes' eye. The old man smiled and and tapped the side of his head. "Well done! You used your brain!" he said.

Spiro picked himself up from the floor. He glowered at Olly. If looks could kill, Olly would have died twice over!

"I-I-I I'll get you, Olly!" Spiro stammered. "I'll get you next time, j-just wait and see."

But Olly knew now that he could beat Spiro again – any time. And Spiro knew it, too.

Chapter Five

The next day, Spiro was out for revenge.

"Come here, you weedy little worm," he spat at Olly. "I've got another parcel for Simonedes and you're going to take it for me, or else."

Kerberos bounded up to Olly, teeth bared and growling. "No one messes with my master!" he seemed to say.

Olly folded his arms and looked the dog in the eyes. Kerberos hesitated and took a step back. Something had changed. Spiro wasn't the boss any more. Kerberos tucked his tail between his legs, trotted back to his master and waited to see what would happen.

Olly walked over to Spiro and put his hand out for the parcel.

"No problem," he said calmly.

"Actually, I was on my way to see Simonedes right now."

All Spiro's bravado blew away in an instant. He didn't seem quite so big or tough any more.

Olly set off for the library. He looked up at the wide blue sky above him and felt the warm spring sunshine on his face. Olly smiled. He felt as if the weight of the world had been lifted off his shoulders.

OLYMPIC FACTS!

DID YOU KNOW...?

The ancient Olympic Games began over 2,700 years ago in Olympia, in southwest Greece.

The ancient Games were were held in honour of Zeus, king of the gods, and were staged every four years at Olympia.

Athletes in the ancient Games usually competed absolutely stark naked!

There were two types of wrestling: *Orthia Pale*, in which you had to throw your opponent to the ground three times; and *Kato Pale*, in which the loser raised a finger to admit defeat.

Today, the modern Olympic Games are still held every four years in a different city around the world.

OLYMPIA

There are more Olympia stories

RUN LIKE THE WIND

WRESTLE TO VICTORY

JUMP FOR GLORY

THROW FOR GOLD

SWIM FOR YOUR LIFE

RACE FOR THE STARS

ON THE BALL

DEADLY TARGET

Get them on Amazon or follow
the links on www.shoorayner.com

Read them all and watch Shoo read them on video.

Follow the links at shoorayner.com

SCAN ME